I CHOOSE CALM

INSPIRATIONAL MANTRAS
AND PRACTICAL MINDFULNESS EXERCISES
FOR PARENTS

ANGELA WOLF

I Choose Calm: Inspirational Mantras
and Practical Mindfulness Exercises for Parents

Angela Wolf

ISBN: 978-1-7347904-0-5 for Paperback
ISBN: 978-1-7347904-1-2 for Ebook

Disclaimer

Paperback ISBN: 978-1-7347904-0-5

Ebook ISBN: 978-1-7347904-1-2

Dedication

I dedicate this book to my son, William, who has taught me more about love and patience than I knew was possible.

CONTENTS

INTRODUCTION

In today's world, mainstream media and social media can overwhelm us with pictures of the perfect family, perfect children, and perfect parents. As a result, by human nature, we might compare those flawlessly staged photos to our own parenting habits. But the truth is that we all experience the same ups and downs of parenthood, even if we're not posting them on social media. We all have a full array of emotions and a long list of responsibilities that can create high levels of stress, causing us to live life on the edge rather than be present in the middle of it.

So what can we do to overcome that anxiety and be more present?

Practice mindfulness.

Practicing mindfulness means creating space to become aware of what is happening internally, like how we feel inside. It is also what is occurring externally with the people and the environment around us. Mindfulness can help us identify the moment we start to experience tenseness or anxiety so that we can make the conscious choice to remain in control when times get tough. With practice, mindfulness can bring us into a calm and present state, enabling us to truly experience all the beauty that parenthood has to offer.

As parents, we hope that our children will be mindful in their everyday lives, yet we don't have a mindfulness regimen of our own to keep us grounded and to provide a positive example for our family. This book is a tool for parents to find inspiration in simple activities and begin to build a daily regimen that will enable us to venture into the present moment, to experience the joy of parenthood, and to mindfully manage the stress that can accompany the joy. (And, for those parents who are interested in helping their children begin a mindfulness routine of their own, the first and most important step is to lead by example. This book is a great place to start.)

Each chapter unlocks a positive mantra that can help all parents —future, new, experienced, single, foster, and even animal parents—to use the power of mindfulness to find peace and acceptance in what can prove to be the most challenging yet rewarding role life can offer. These aren't your classic Sanskrit mantras but, rather, practical life mantras that are divided into three sections: love, acceptance, and inspiration. All are vital to successful parenting, and some more than others, depending on the moment.

Love is the nonnegotiable foundation to any parent-child relationship. Yet, self-love is just as important, if not more important, because only with a sense of genuine love for ourselves can we truly open our hearts to give love and receive love from others. Self-love can come in many forms, such as allowing ourselves to take a break and practice self-care, to finding the peace and happiness that can only truly reside in our hearts. Gratitude and forgiveness are also key components of living a balanced life, and these can only be felt fully and honestly when love is present.

Acceptance is a necessary process by which we give ourselves space to be the best we can be while acknowledging that nothing and no one is perfect. It gives us the ability to be unique and messy and make mistakes while knowing that we are doing our best to be good parents and good people. It offers peace of mind about the stresses of life and frees us from the worries that do us more harm than good.

In this book, I offer space for gratitude during many of the mindful moments. If a sincere feeling of gratitude is not accessible in the moment, acceptance of a feeling or a situation is a good alternative. Embracing acceptance might require you to be open to any emotions that need to be fully felt and processed in order to enable your energy to move and for acceptance to surface. I challenge you to open your heart and your mind to that experience as a path to true acceptance.

Inspiration gives us the hope that we need to keep going after a difficult day. It lifts our spirits and reminds us that the choice is ours to choose patience, to choose peace, to choose calm, even when we've hit our wit's end. It encourages us to use a mindful response when a parenting challenge arises rather than an impulsive reaction.

I don't claim to have authored any of these mantras—except one that my dad has been telling me for as long as I can remember: "All you can do is the best you do, and the best you can do is enough." But I share them here because they've helped me, and hopefully they will also help you. I encourage you to write those that resonate the most with you and put them in places that will inspire you beyond the borders of this book. Some might even become part of your daily routine or be shared with your family. For that, we can thank the creative minds from where these inspirational words came.

The mindfulness activities that accompany the mantras are a mix of simple techniques, like conscious breathing, visualization, meditation, and energy awareness to help you cultivate love, acceptance, and inspiration. These are based on research, mindfulness coursework, and my own experiences. I work to incorporate these into my life when appropriate, but like every one of us, I'm also a work in progress, still learning how and when to make them work for me.

Some of the activities are best practiced when you can find a simple moment of peace for yourself, while some of the activities are meant to be shared with your family. Some are practical, while others draw on what might be newer concepts to you, such as working with your energy and using your imagination to help you visualize. I suggest trying a new one each day or week and eventually selecting a few that are good fits for your routine.

Soon you will likely find yourself right here, right now, in the present moment. You will be able to share more meaningful moments with your family, focus on the joys of life, sift out the noise that does not support a focused life, and remain aware of the ups and downs while letting yourself process them fully without judgment. The path to a mindful life isn't easy, especially as a parent, but it's a path that can lead to richer experiences with those whom we love the most.

A Note about Practicing Mindful Moments

Everyone knows that being a parent isn't easy, but it doesn't have to be overwhelming in the moment. Tools like these mantras and mindfulness exercises are useful to support your *choice* to be the most grounded person you can be with the thoughtful responses during the most trying situations.

Even with the desire to choose to respond thoughtfully, we all have our good days and our chaotic days. And that's okay. Self-compassion is a key ingredient to getting through the chaotic days intact with lessons learned.

I suggest you try these exercises when it suits you—in the morning, in the heat of the moment, or before you go to bed. Every person is different. Every parent is different. Every day is different. So, be kind to yourself as you work through this book. It will likely take repetition to really feel grounded with many of these "mindful moments," and that's okay.

Along the way, feel free to make them your own by changing them or adding to them, as it feels right for you. They are merely meant as a launching point to bring mindfulness into your daily routine and, ideally, to make mindfulness a habit in your responses as a parent and a human being.

A Note about Practicing Mindfulness with Your Children

I've offered suggestions about which mindfulness exercises might be appropriate to share with your children. When doing so, it's helpful to remind yourself that they might view an experience, a mantra, or a mindfulness exercise differently than you. And that's okay. I encourage you to ask for their perspectives about how a situation feels, what a mantra means to them, and how they can make a mindfulness exercise work for them.

Practicing mindfulness together can be a unique bonding experience and a valuable method of learning more about your children. As a children's meditation teacher, I am constantly learning from my students about how to make lessons more fun or easier to understand. I consider those suggestions as gifts that help me as a teacher, adult, and parent to learn more about their perspectives and to forge more meaningful connections with them in the moment.

Another suggestion for bringing these mindfulness activities to younger children is to make the exercises as tactile as possible. This can be done through the use of purposeful movement. When cued to take a deep breath, make the movement palpable by spreading your arms out wide on an inhale and bringing them back to your heart on an exhale. When prompted to think of a word or write a list, they might choose to draw a picture. Drawing might also be helpful when describing how they feel in the moment.

The use of relaxing music might also be a good way to signal that a mindful moment is beginning. I like to use essential oils or incense when I meditate to guide my brain into a different space. In the same way, we can help children enter the world of mindfulness by offering a change in scenery through a change in space, sound, or smell.

Most of all, I encourage you to honor whatever comes up for them during the exercises as you help them create their own lasting mindfulness habits to carry through the journey of life.

Section I: Love

"Being a family means you are a part of something very wonderful. It means you will love and be loved for the rest of your life."

—*Lisa Weed*

LOVE

Love is the foundation for a strong family bond. It connects us to find joy in the good times and supports us through the rough times. The following mantras encourage you to practice love for your family and also—and some would argue more important—for yourself.

Authentically showing ourselves love enables us to focus on what's most important and to find peace, happiness, gratitude, and forgiveness in our hearts.

CHAPTER 1

I Give Love
and
I Am Loved

Mindful Reflection

You might have heard the saying "All you need is love." Being a parent is an outstanding way to help us understand just how true that saying is and how our ability to give and receive love can critically affect the lives of our children and significant others. The mantra "I give love and I am loved" goes a bit further to acknowledge that love is a two-way energy exchange. Our ability to feel comfortable with the energy of love flowing in and out of our hearts, in addition to our belief that we are worthy of love, can make a difference in how well we give and receive love in general.

I encourage you to let this mantra sit with you for a time and feel it. Don't think about; *feel* it. How does it make you feel? *Insight: Sometimes how a mantra makes us feel can be as enlightening as how we use it to calm or inspire us.* Does it feel natural, or is there a hesitation as you feel it? Are you as comfortable receiving love as you are giving love? Without an open heart, ready and willing to receive the love that others share with you, it can be difficult to share your true love with others.

Mindful Moment

Time: 3–5 minutes
What You Need: A quiet space

1. Find a comfortable seat and take a deep breath in through your nose and out through your mouth.
2. Sit quietly for a minute with your eyes closed and maintain your natural breath in and out through your nose.
3. After a minute of focusing on your breath, imagine seeing yourself sitting in front of you looking peaceful, happy, and full of love. Smile … this is your true self shining through.
4. Now imagine yourself sitting in front of you stressed out and having a bad day, feeling defeated, and not especially worthy of love. Smile … this is your true self needing love from you.

5. Take a deep breath in and imagine a pink light emerging from the center of your heart and surrounding the defeated, stressed-out version of you sitting across from yourself. Feel the light get warmer and brighter until you feel full of love. Slowly see the stressed-out version of you starting to feel comforted and filling up with this pink light of love. Continue until you are both smiling. (Remember, your imagination is critical here; treat your image of yourself as though it is really you, and you'll be amazed at how your imagination can help you share love and positive energy with yourself.)
6. Once you are both smiling, take a deep breath and say, "I give love and I am loved."
7. *Bonus: When you have a few more moments in the future, repeat this for each member of your family, and see how it might change your perception of your relationship and possibly even their behavior.*

CHAPTER 2

My Child Is Loved

Mindful Reflection

Our primary job as parents is to raise our children with love as we keep them safe, healthy, and happy. As children grow, they learn over time how to process their emotions constructively ... or we can help teach them to do so through mindfulness! Yet, throughout the learning process, they're bound to throw a tantrum or lash out in frustration. That's part of childhood, but it doesn't mean it's easy to manage. *Suggestion: You can also read the mantra "My child is only a child" (see chapter 14) and perform that mindfulness exercise when needed.*

As parents, we often receive these situations as though we've done something wrong, or we allow ourselves to get embarrassed by the reactions of bystanders who might have a front seat to the tantrum. It's during those times of great frustration or disappointment that it's helpful to get back to basics about the relationship with our children.

Despite our children acting like children, we have the power to remind ourselves that we are doing our best at our most important job— to raise them with love. A moment of self-compassion can shift our perspective about the gravity of the situation; it can also enable us to respond thoughtfully and with compassion to our child, thereby serving as a good example.

Mindful Moment

Time: 1 minute
What You Need: An intention for awareness in the moment but no need for a quiet space

1. When you need a shift in perspective during a tough moment, simply pause and come to your breath. Make a conscious effort to focus on your breath as it enters and exits your nostrils, thereby shifting your focus, briefly, and creating space from the current situation.

2. Imagine a gold light pouring out of your heart and connecting to your child's heart. If it helps, close your eyes and put your hand to your heart to feel that connection of sincere love.
3. Breathe in deeply. Silently say, "My child is loved." With the exhale, release any tension you might be holding. *Suggestion: Repeat this step several times, if necessary.*
4. With a new perspective and a renewed sense of compassion, continue with a thoughtful response to the situation. A hug might be good idea. Or, if not possible, a compassionate tone of voice, an ear to listen, or a smile is appropriate.

CHAPTER 3

Everyone Shows Love in Different Ways

Mindful Reflection

One could argue that love is the foundation of a parent-child relationship. However, the ways in which we show each other love can vary so much that we might overlook the little things our children do to show us love in their own, unique ways.

Oftentimes, if we allow ourselves to maintain an open heart, be present in the moment, and remain curiously aware of the things our children do and say, we are able to fully receive and accept the love they're sharing. It might be a hug or a kiss. It might be a smile or a kind word. It could even be a temper tantrum or a moment of silence instead of an anticipated response.

Our children communicate with us in so many ways, oftentimes not as we expect or wish. But even the toughest moments can be their opportunity to show us how much they appreciate us, if we are open to listening and leaving behind any notions of what love *should* look like.

I suggest first trying this exercise alone as a visualization of a past situation that might benefit from a thoughtful review. Then, over time, it can be brought into the moment. It is especially helpful for parents of older children who are going through hormonal changes and might not be showing love as they have in the past.

Mindful Moment

Time: 1–3 minutes
What You Need: It's helpful to have a quiet space, but this can also be used in the moment, as needed

1. First, offer yourself the space to receive love. This can be done mentally by saying, "I love myself. I love my child." Or, it can be done physically by placing your hand over your heart.
2. Next, take a deep breath in, as you feel your heart fill with a warm white light. As you exhale, allow yourself to release that white light to share love with others who are present.

3. Now, think of how your child shows love. Start with the things that might be obvious, such as hugs, kisses, and loving words. Then, move on to other things that might be communicating love in a different way, such as asking for help or advice. Next, move on to any other actions that might even be confusing or frustrating. Allow yourself to feel these experiences rather than just think about them. How does your heart feel when you envision them? Do you sense love? Do you sense a call for help that might imply love and trust is present? How can you show love in return? *Insight: As you allow yourself to be mindful of the feeling of love and to fully process the request for love, you might realize that it is best to return the love in a nonconventional way.*
4. Smile, you are loved. You receive love, even incognito.
5. Now, take a deep breath and repeat step 1.

CHAPTER 4

Peace Is Found from Within

Mindful Reflection

Amid the internal and external chaos that can accompany daily life, it is essential to create a place of solace to find peace. Many would agree that inner peace is the most important kind, as it tends to create a ripple effect in how you treat yourself, how you treat others, and the example that you set for those who look up to you. What more important example can we set for our children than the ability to find peace from within. But how do we do it?

Mindful Moment

Time: 3–5 minutes
What You Need: A quiet space

1. First, find your breath, and begin to slow down and come to the present moment. Feel the ground or floor below you supporting you, even through times of chaos. With a deep breath, silently thank the universe for guiding you through times of chaos in the past, as it will continue to do in the future.
2. Next, take a minute or two to imagine your perfect place of peace. Maybe it's sitting by a fireplace reading a book. Maybe it's relaxing on a beach or sitting in the grass, barefoot, feeling the breeze on your face. Maybe it's lying in bed with your family snuggling all around you, giggling, talking, and enjoying the moment.
3. Think about how you feel while in that place, and think about where in your body you feel it. Do you feel comfortable, happy, energetic, or maybe relaxed? Do you feel it in your heart, your head, your belly, or elsewhere? Do you smell or hear anything as part of the experience?
4. Feel yourself immersed in the experience, and let the feeling of comfort and peace slowly fill your heart.
5. Once your heart is full, slowly come back to your breath and smile. This feeling of a full heart is always available to you when you need to find a moment of peace during an especially chaotic time.

6. *Suggestion: Give this place and this feeling a code word, like "peace." When a day comes around that steals your inner peace and overwhelms you—and, let's be honest, we all have them—use your code word and your breath to come back to this place. Sit with it for as long as you need. You can also teach your children this mindfulness exercise to help them manage their own anxiety.*

CHAPTER 5

Happiness Is an Inside Job

Mindful Reflection

So much of our lives revolves around seeking happiness and validation from external sources. It starts when we're young and encouraged to get that star or sticker or good grade to validate our hard work. And it follows us through life into our jobs, into our relationships, and certainly into our view of others' lives through social media.

Many of us have heard that happiness comes from within, and deep down we know it's true. But it's almost impossible to break through programming that has been deeply coded into our psyches since before we can remember. It's through daily reminders and mindful practices that we can begin to chip away at our craving for external praise and be truly happy with ourselves for who we are *being* as human beings and not what we are *doing*.

Mindful Moment

Time: 5 minutes
What You Need: A quiet space and possibly a pencil and paper
Note: This is fun to do with your children too

1. First, smile. Even the simple act of smiling can make you happier. This is something I like to visit at the beginning and end a lot of my mindful activities with. Don't forget the power of a genuine smile.
2. Next, think of something you can see that makes you happy. It doesn't have to be something you can see at the moment; it can be something you've seen before that makes you happy, such as a sunrise. Take a breath in and pause to imprint this sight in your memory as a source of happiness. As you breathe out, think, *I choose happiness.*
3. Then, think of something you can taste that makes you happy; this one shouldn't be too difficult for most of us. Again, use your breath to imprint this taste in your memory and choose happiness.

4. Next, find something you can touch that makes you happy. Use your breath to stamp it in your memory and acknowledge your choice for happiness.

5. Next, find something you can smell that makes you happy, such as fresh-baked chocolate chip cookies. Repeat the breathing exercise, and maybe taste those cookies at the same time.

6. Next, think of something you can hear that makes you happy, like laughing or singing a song with your kids, and repeat the breathing exercise one last time.

7. *Bonus: Over the next couple of days, seek out each of those experiences, so you can experience that happiness with all of your senses.*

8. Finally, and most important, create a list of three words that describe you and make you happy. These can be caring, authentic, and silly, or any crazy words that truly give you reason to be happy with yourself. On days when you start to feel your inner happiness fading, find those words, and take three deep breaths as you say them silently and smile. Happiness still resides in your heart.

CHAPTER 6

Joy Begins with an Open Heart

Mindful Reflection

People often think of children when they think of joy. Children seem so naturally able to find the fun and the joy in everyday activities, like walking in the rain or sitting in a sandbox. It seems as though they don't need to look for opportunities to be joyful; joy finds them. But finding joy can be a choice we all make in our daily lives.

From expressing gratitude for each day while looking at the sunrise to enjoying the innocence and smiles of our children, it is possible to find joy sprinkled throughout our days if we know where to find it and we allow ourselves to feel it. Having an open heart (and, with it, a foundation of self-love) can be the key to unlocking the gift of joy in our lives and in our hearts.

Mindful Moment

Time: 1–3 minutes
What You Need: A quiet space
Note: This is fun to do with your children too

1. Close your eyes. Take a few deep breaths.
2. Bring your hands to your heart, and imagine a magic key in your hands that is warm and shining bright like a star in the sky.
3. With a big breath in, imagine yourself using this key to unlock your heart. Feel the power of love emanating throughout your body, filling you with a pink light that shoots out from your heart and the crown of your head.
4. Now, think of something that brings you pure joy. It can be as simple as a smile from someone you love.
5. Ask yourself where you feel this joy. Is it in your heart? In your head? In your hands? In your smile?
6. Now, imagine a white light bursting from the place in your body where you feel joy.
7. Bring both hands to the place on your body where you experience joy, and smile.

8. *Suggestion: In the future, when you need joy in the moment, bring your hands to your heart and to the place where you find joy, if it's elsewhere on your body. And don't forget to smile!*

CHAPTER 7

Sometimes Putting Yourself First Isn't Selfish but Necessary

Mindful Reflection

This is a great mantra for starting a healthy habit that puts you first when needed. If you've ever been an exhausted parent—and chances are you have—you know how difficult it is to care for someone else when you have little energy to spare. Without a full cup of your own, you don't have enough to give to those you love, and you might not be surprised to learn that they can often tell when you're running low on fuel.

Establishing a mindful habit to reward or refresh yourself can give you the extra fuel you need to be the best parent possible. And, it can set a good example for your children about how important it is to honor yourself and your energy.

Mindful Moment

Time: 3–5 minutes
What You Need: A quiet space

1. First, close your eyes and take a deep breath. As you continue to breathe deeply, take a minute to give gratitude for your time as a parent, including this moment to stop and breathe.
2. Next, spend a minute to think about everything you do, day in and day out, to support your family. Imagine that each of those "things" you do is a flower in the garden. See the garden getting fuller and more beautiful because of the love and care you bring to it by watering it every day.
3. Now, think of the things you do for yourself. These can be things that you need to do, like showering or sleeping (or meditating!), or things that you do to treat yourself for all your hard work, like watching your favorite TV show or spending a night with friends. See each of those things also as a garden. That garden might not be as full as the family garden, but it's also important to keep it watered each day.

4. Imagine one thing you don't normally do to treat yourself but that you would really benefit from doing for yourself. This could be taking a bubble bath after a long day or simply adding one minute to your morning or night routine to journal each day. Imagine yourself planting that flower and watering it, and smile at how beautiful it looks in your garden. This is a new habit you can add to your daily or weekly routine, or even just to your emergency self-care kit when your energy levels are low.

5. *Suggestion: Consider making a habit of visiting your family garden and your personal garden each week to make sure you're watering all the flowers and to think about any new flowers you might like to plant.*

CHAPTER 8

It Is Okay to Say No to Unnecessary Crazy

Mindful Reflection

Boundaries are an essential part of maintaining sanity, especially for parents, and they're an important part of self-love. While you might have been able to balance commitments for family, work, friends, fun, and self-care before parenthood, it can be downright impossible to fit everything in and maintain any sort of balance once you have others to take care of. But how can you eliminate the "crazy," unnecessary demands to maintain space for life's most important commitments?

Sometimes planning your day or week will help you prioritize the most important demands, and anything else that comes along is icing on the cake. But, there are times when unexpected requests come your way and a mindful moment can help you tap into your intuition to determine if it's really something you should take on or decide that it's "unnecessary crazy."

Mindful Moment

Time: 3–5 minutes
What You Need: A quiet space and possibly a pencil and paper

1. To tap into your intuition at times when you might be stretched too thin, close your eyes, take a few deep breaths, and take a quick inventory of what you have on your plate.
2. Ask yourself the following question: "Do I have enough time to meet my basic family responsibilities without unreasonable stress *and* have space set aside for self-care, even for a few minutes at the beginning or the end of the day?"
3. *Suggestion: Think back to the self-care garden in the mindfulness exercise for chapter 7, "Sometimes putting yourself first isn't selfish but necessary," to determine if your self-care needs are being supported.*
4. Now, be mindful of the response: If the answer was "no," then there is likely an opportunity to say "no" to at least one commitment you have. But what if you have no choice? Then reprioritizing your demands and pushing one or two until the next day might be your only option.

5. If the answer was "yes," then consider how your stomach feels when you think about taking on the new task or request. If it feels upset or tense, it's probably something that is not a good idea to take on, at least at the time.

But what if the challenge is not about whether you should take it on but, rather, if you know you can't or shouldn't, how to actually say "no" to the request? As parents, oftentimes we feel like we must say "yes" to everything or else we're not meeting the expectations of a "good parent." But oftentimes the parents who are happiest and have the happiest families are the ones who are the best at setting boundaries and saying "no," kindly, when needed.

If simply saying "no" doesn't feel authentic to you, try saying, "I don't have time, but I wish I could help" or "Thanks for thinking of me ... maybe next time." Consider it an honest way to love yourself and your family enough to protect their boundaries and prioritize your needs. And, if you say it with love in your heart, you can feel it in your gut as the right decision and in your heart as an act of love for the people you love, including yourself.

Just remember, you should also be open to others who are protecting their boundaries when they say "no" to your request. Respond with the same understanding and loving energy that you would request in response.

CHAPTER 9

I Give Myself Permission to Slow Down

Mindful Reflection

Sometimes the best form of self-care is showing yourself love by allowing yourself to slow down and enjoy all the hard work you've already done. Sometimes it means just being realistic about what can actually be done in one day without losing your sanity or giving away all your energy.

On Sundays, I like to create a plan for my week and then revisit those to-do lists each morning to recalibrate as needed. I'll admit that sometimes I put way too much on my plate, and it can seem like a herculean task to accomplish everything on that day's to-do list. This is when I have to remind myself that the most important thing is to *be* not to *do*.

What do I want to *be* that day? Productive? How about at peace and happy? The power to *be* is something I can control from within with practice. If I want to *be* the happy, kind, supportive, and best parent I can be, then it means I'll have to first make sure my cup is full, and then I can help others.

By starting with what I want to be, it helps me to be more realistic with my time and double-check myself when I am creating my to-do list. Instead of getting carried away with a list of "nice-to-haves," I ask myself: "What are the one or two things I must accomplish today? Do I have time for a nice-to-have? How do those things help me be the person I strive to be? If they do not, do they deserve a spot on my to-do list, or can they be delegated or reprioritized?

By freeing myself from every single thing I think I need to *do*, I am better able to focus on the most important tasks that help me *be* happy and healthy.

Mindful Moment

Time: 1–3 minutes, preferably at the beginning of the day.
What You Need: A quiet space and possibly a pencil and paper

1. Start by sitting for at least a minute with mindful breathing and posing a question: "What do I want to *be* this day?"
2. Allow words, ideas, or feelings to emerge organically from your subconscious. Collect them without judgment, and when you feel as though you've allowed yourself to explore this question fully, close with a few seconds of gratitude for allowing yourself to *be* just as you are and nothing more in this present moment.
3. When it's time to plan out your day or week, use those concepts from your meditation as a litmus test to prioritize what you really plan to accomplish.
4. Don't forget to celebrate and show gratitude at the end of the day or week once you do accomplish what you'd planned!

CHAPTER 10

I Honor Myself and the Love I Bring to My Family

Mindful Reflection

As you're well aware, being a parent can often be a thankless job. As a play-time supervisor, chef, taxi driver, and VIP snuggler, there are more than enough hats in this job to exhaust and overwhelm you, but there's rarely a big "thank you" waiting for you at the end of the day.

Maintaining the intrinsic motivation to be the best parent you can be is a critical piece of the puzzle. However, if you're mindful and grateful for the opportunity to take this wild ride, you'll find that there are kudos all around if you know where to look.

Mindful Moment

Time: 3–5 minutes
What You Need: An intention for awareness in the moment but no need for a quiet space

1. Wherever you are, whatever you're doing, take a second to consciously connect with your breath and bring your awareness to the present moment. Really focus on the feeling of your chest rising and your belly expanding when you inhale, and feel your whole body relax as you exhale.
2. Start to notice the sounds around you. Start to notice anything you smell or feel. Does anything pop out to you, now that you're paying close attention?
3. Now that you're grounded in the moment, take a second to smile and thank yourself for all that you do, day in and day out. Yes, you're giving yourself credit, and that's the first step to being open to allowing others to do the same or even to being open to noticing when others are already doing so.
4. Look at your child and think about the phases you've watched come and go so far. Maybe you have a newborn and are excited to see your child roll over for the first time. Maybe you have a toddler and are excited to see your child talking or walking. Maybe you have a child who is in school and learning new things. Or maybe you have an adolescent

and are excited to see the seeds of independence sowing. Whatever the stage, think about the progress your child has made and all of the hard work you've put into making that possible. Smile, breathe deeply, and say, "thank you."

5. Now think about the many obstacles you've helped your child or your family overcome since becoming a parent. No matter what stage of parenting you're in, there is some form of challenge awaiting. Maybe it's your child learning to crawl, learning to read, or feeling confident in going to the first day of school. Whatever the challenge, you have been there as a cheerleader to help your child overcome that obstacle. Smile, breathe deeply, and say, "thank you."

6. Now think about the many adventures and challenges that lie ahead for your child. The big game, the final exam, the first kiss. As you breathe deeply, tune into your heart and feel the energy within. Know within your heart that you'll do anything you can to support your child in each step of the upcoming journey. Smile, breathe deeply, and say, "thank you."

7. Finally, look into your child's eyes and give him or her a big, heartfelt hug. Smile, and say "thank you." Thank your child for the opportunity to offer your support as you journey through life together. Not everyone is granted their wish to be a parent, if they so choose. With that reflection in mind, one last time, say "thank you," and hear those words echo from your heart to your child's heart and back to your own heart, filling it with gratitude and warmth that will guide the way.

CHAPTER 11

Gratitude Is the Gift That Keeps on Giving

Mindful Reflection

Gratitude is one of the greatest gifts you can give yourself. Many people choose to begin or end their day with thoughts of gratitude, and that can be one of the most potent mindfulness practices possible.

If you believe in the law of attraction or even just the power of positive thinking, then sharing a "thank you" for all the positives in your life—love, safety, security, nourishment, and each day you are granted the opportunity to be alive and to be a parent—can be a powerful means of cultivating even more fortune.

Mindful Moment

Time: 3–5 minutes
What You Need: A quiet space and a view of the stars, if possible
Note: This is fun to do with your children too

This is a simple gratitude meditation that can offer perspective on even the most stressful days. It's best to find a few minutes of peace, if possible, for this exercise, even if it's just the minute or two before your head hits the pillow at the end of the day. This is also a wonderful exercise for teaching your children the importance of gratitude.

1. First, find your breath. Take three deep breaths in, and with each exhale, imagine yourself sitting outside in the moonlight and looking up at the night sky. Each star you see in the sky is something to be thankful for.
2. *Bonus if you can actually be outside looking at the stars, but using your imagination can be just as powerful.*
3. For the first star you see, give thanks for something basic that you enjoy each day and might not even think of, such as having enough food and water. Continue giving thanks to that star for as many essentials as you can think of, such as having a home, having clothing to wear, etc.
4. Next, find a star to give thanks for things that your family can bring you, such as laughter and memories. Feel each of these in your heart as you think of them.

5. The next star you see can be used to give thanks for things that you enjoy that others might not have the opportunity to enjoy, such as time to meditate, the physical ability (and, let's face it, the time in the day) to work out, or even the capability to juggle groceries while you tie a little shoe and listen to the story of your child's day.

6. Another star can be used to give thanks for things you do that everyone can do but might not take the time to do, such as giving a smile to someone who is feeling down or even giving a warm hug to your child when he or she is feeling hurt or frustrated.

7. You can continue finding stars and finding new categories for which to give thanks. If you can't find another star but have more gratitude to share, imagine another star in the sky. Each time you look at the stars in the future, you can revisit that gift of gratitude, and it will, indeed, keep on giving you the opportunity to rejoice about all the wonderful things that you have and that you are.

CHAPTER 12

I Forgive Others as I Forgive Myself

Mindful Reflection

Forgiveness is an incredibly powerful force that can free the heart and release the soul from bondage. Forgiveness is also an important component of self-love. To love someone else enough to forgive them of their transgressions, you must have a deep love for yourself and also be able to forgive yourself.

That can be difficult to do with a job as demanding as parenthood, where mistakes are an inherent part of the process. But without forgiveness, we are destined (or doomed) into a spiral of guilt that will not serve us and certainly will not serve our children.

Mindful Moment

Time: 5 minutes
What You Need: A quiet space

1. Close your eyes and imagine an instance for which you would like to forgive yourself.
2. Think about what happened—what you thought, said, and did. Try not to place judgment, but instead, think of the situation as an objective bystander documenting what you see.
3. Think about how your actions affected you and others. Again, avoid placing judgment but, instead, put yourself in the other person's (or people's) shoes to understand the impact.
4. Think about what you might have done differently if you had taken the time to be mindful of your response and, if needed, given space to the situation before responding.
5. Now, envision yourself in your mind sitting peacefully and meditating on forgiveness.
6. Envision yourself being surrounded by a circle of pink light, and then imagine yourself in that circle of pink light floating toward your heart and being absorbed into your heart.
7. Take a deep breath and imagine all the good things you've thought, said, and done that have made a positive impact on yourself and others.

8. Tell yourself that you are doing the best you can and that you have made a mistake. Take a deep breath in and say, "I forgive you." And as you breathe out, say, "I love you."

9. Then, take a deep breath and think of the situation again. If you still feel as though you harbor resentment toward yourself, repeat the exercise. Once you can feel in your heart as though you have truly forgiven yourself, take a deep breath and smile.

10. *Bonus: Perform this activity for a situation for which you would like to forgive someone else. Think of what they might have said or done. Envision them in a circle of pink light. Absorb that pink light into your heart, and forgive them with your breath, your words, your heart, and with a smile.*

Section II: Acceptance

"Accept—then act. Whatever the present moment contains, accept it as if you had chosen it. Always work with it, not against it."

—*Eckhart Tolle*

ACCEPTANCE

The path to self-love and true happiness crosses the path of acceptance. Accepting one's self, one's failures, and one's choices are just as important as accepting that of another. Acceptance enables us to embrace our reality and authentically forgive ourselves and others to release that which no longer serves us.

It reminds us that we, as human beings, are neither perfect nor should we strive to *be*. It grants us the space to *be* ourselves and the choice to *do* our best on this journey of parenthood.

CHAPTER 13

Accept What Is, Let Go of What Was, Believe in What Will Be

Mindful Reflection

Acceptance is a choice. It's a choice to acknowledge and make space for the good, the bad, and the ugly, and then to move on. It can also be viewed as a gift to ourselves and others to forgive mistakes or transgressions and continue to grow in our relationships. One could even say that acceptance is also critical to sanity in parenthood. Without it, we can get mired in guilt and shame that, in the end, won't serve our cause to be the best parents and people we can be.

Unfortunately, acceptance isn't generally on the easy path in life. It takes effort, humility, and sometimes courage. Thankfully, mindfulness is an excellent tool to home in on a situation in the present or even after it's happened and to give it the understanding and, ultimately, the space required to help us accept, release, and move on.

Mindful Moment

Time: 3–5 minutes
What You Need: A quiet space
Note: This can be helpful to teach to older children too

1. Take a deep breath in and think of a mistake you've made as a parent. As you breathe out, imagine sending that thought to your heart. Feel your heart absorbing that thought in a bright pink light.
2. With your next breath in, bring your hands to your heart. As you breathe out, say, "I forgive myself. I love myself. I release this thought to the universe. I will continue to do the best that I can."
3. Smile. Take three slow, deep, thoughtful breaths.
4. On your next breath in, think of something difficult that you live with but cannot change, at least not for now. As you breathe out, send that thought to the bright light in your heart.

5. With your next breath in, bring your hands to your heart, and as you breathe out, say, "I accept this. I love myself. I will continue to do the best that I can."
6. Smile. Take three more slow, deep breaths.
7. On your next breath in, imagine you and your family living in pure joy despite you not being perfect. Send that joyful thought to your heart on your exhale.
8. As you breathe out, bring your hands to your heart, and with the exhale, say, "I love myself. I love my family. I cherish the joy that each moment can bring."
9. Smile. Finish with three slow, deep breaths.
10. *Suggestion: Repeat this each day as needed to accept, release, and believe.*

CHAPTER 14

My Child Is Only a Child

Mindful Reflection

With all the expectations that seem to be placed on children these days, it is easy to overlook that they are just children and still learning their place in this world. The impact of social media can also set a high bar on the achievements or even the behavior of children to be well behaved at all times, because what we see on social media is generally the highlight reel of someone else's life. As we know, however, children still experience complex emotions and sometimes lack the capabilities or the emotional intelligence tools to express those emotions constructively.

Giving our child the opportunity to make mistakes and learn is critical, just as you hopefully had the opportunity to do. That's why this mantra "My child is only a child" can be so powerful. It stops us in our tracks when we're frustrated that our child's actions are not aligning to our expectations. It can even be a good time to reminisce about the lessons you've learned over the years.

How have you come to be the person you are today? What mistakes have you made and hard lessons have you learned that helped you grow stronger? What mistakes are your children making, and are they able to stop and learn from each of them?

They're not simple questions, and the answers are likely just as complex. But this perspective is an important part of accepting our children—and their mistakes—as part of the experience. It doesn't mean ignore the mistakes; it means acknowledge, learn from, and release them as only true acceptance can facilitate.

Mindful Moment

Time: 5–10 minutes
What You Need: A quiet space and possibly a pencil and paper

This is a good example of a mindfulness exercise that can be shared with your children. It's simple, but it's powerful and effective. When your children make a mistake or lash out in frustration, you can be the source of mindful learning for them.

Suggestion: It is recommended to try this on your own to manage your own frustration after your child's mistake or outburst and, over time, use the sense of self-love and awareness that you generate from your own practice to bring it to your child to help him or her in the moment.

It's important to note that it's critical not to force an answer during this exercise. Simply breathe and let the answers float into your mind. The same is true as you help your children discover their own answers. Let them find their way through their breath, through their thoughts, and into their intuition for guidance.

The experience can be enlightening and bring you and your child closer even in the face of an outburst or incident. Over time, taking the time to pause and reflect *during* the incident and potentially change the outcome can be lifechanging.

1. First, it's critical to acknowledge that we all make mistakes. This is something each of us has likely had to tell ourselves in the past. If not, now is the time to start. It can give us the space we need to step back from our thoughts or actions and reflect as an observer.
2. Next, establish a conscious breathing pattern to decrease your heart rate and bring yourself into the "now" rather than reliving the past action. You could try a simple breathing exercise, such as three-count inhale, one-count pause, three-count exhale, one-count pause. Or, my favorite way to engage the parasympathetic nervous system is to lengthen your exhale by a count or two longer than the exhale. For example, three-count inhale, one-count pause, four- or five-count exhale, one-count pause.
3. Next, while continuing with your conscious breathing pattern, perform a quick body scan, starting with the top of your head and ending at your toes. Where do you feel tension, tightness, or discomfort? Breathe into those spaces while saying, "Everything will be all right."

4. Now you're in a better place to step back and think about, (a) what happened, (b) your contribution and reaction to the event, (c) how you might have made a different decision in the moment, and (d) where there is a valuable life lesson to be learned.
5. As you briefly ponder the life lesson, take a long, deep breath to inhale the lesson and exhale any judgment you might be holding regarding the incident or mistake. Say, "I forgive you. Thank you for the life lesson."
6. With your next breath, tense your entire body and then relax completely.
7. *Bonus: Perform another body scan to ensure you are no longer holding tension. If you are, take a few deep breaths and repeat the tense-and-relax exercise as needed.*
8. Smile and return to your normal breath. Consider journaling about the lesson you learned.

CHAPTER 15

Children Are the Most Important Work

Mindful Reflection

For working parents, it can be difficult to balance a career and family life. That challenge is something that many, or dare I say, *most* parents experience at some point in their lives. One usually comes at the expense of the other. This is where acceptance, self-compassion, and perspective come into play.

Acceptance is helpful when it comes to creating space to better understand the struggle. With acceptance, we can acknowledge the dynamics of the balancing act. Sure, there sometimes exists the opportunity to improve our planning and better coordinate our activities to make more room for our family and ourselves. But the balancing act will always be there in some respect, and just accepting that can be helpful, as can reminding ourselves that we are not alone in the struggle.

We can then take the opportunity to offer ourselves self-compassion for all the hard work we put into each priority in our lives. One of my favorite mantras is "All you can do is the best you can do, and the best you can do is enough." That mantra (see chapter 31) inspires me to use self-compassion and to keep going, even when I feel like I'm not fully succeeding at every demand that life throws my way.

Once we offer ourselves self-compassion, it's time to re-establish our perspective about what's most important in life. Dr. John Trainer said, "Children are not a distraction from more important work. They are the most important work." Unfortunately, society hasn't always celebrated a healthy, happy, well-taken-care-of child as much as it does a fancy work title.

We know down deep that the health, happiness, and safety of our family is our most important job. Yes, the paycheck from work is often what enables us to create a healthy, happy, and safe environment in which to raise our children. However, in the moment, when our heart is heavy and our email inbox is filling up, we have the power to breathe and regain the perspective about our most important work and the impact it has on our lives and the lives of our children.

Mindful Moment

Time: 1–3 minutes
What You Need: An intention for awareness in the moment but no need for a quiet space

1. This is a simple and quick exercise that is meant to be performed immediately in the moment when the struggle is real. Take a deep breath in through your nose and let out an audible breath through your mouth.
2. Feel your connection to the ground or seat. Feel your chest rise and fall with each breath and your belly expand and contract. Allow yourself to briefly acknowledge the world around you and the world inside you. Maintain this sense of deep awareness during the next few steps.
3. With your next breath, tell yourself silently, "I am okay. This is difficult. But, I am okay in this moment."
4. Next, bring a hand to your heart (or imagine doing so, if you're not able to in the moment). With a deep breath, tell yourself silently, "I'm doing the best I can."
5. Finally, realign your perspective. If you're with your family at the moment, make eye contact with your child, if possible. (This can be repeated for each child). And if you're not with your family, close your eyes briefly and conjure the image of your child.
6. Pause to establish the energetic connection that brings you back to the perspective about life's priorities. With your next breath, tell yourself silently, "Children are my most important work."
7. *Bonus: With your perspective in place, you might choose to share additional time with your child in the moment and, in doing so, be proud that you are performing your most important work.*

CHAPTER 16

We Are Not Defined by Our Worst Moments

Mindful Reflection

Parenthood can feel like a roller coaster. There are highs and lows, and sometimes they happen within seconds of one another. One thing is certain: all parents have been frustrated and out of patience at one time or another. It turns out that raising little humans can be really tough, especially when they're doing what kids are supposed to be doing—experimenting, pushing the boundaries, and learning about the world and themselves.

Although rough times are inherently part of the process, we have the opportunity to consciously make a choice about how we *respond* to our feelings of frustration rather than choosing to *react* with anger through our words or actions. One of the biggest values of having our own daily meditation or mindfulness practice is that we have the ability to sense our emotions before they take over us.

We can use mindfulness to trace our emotions as soon as they sneak up—sweaty palms, warm temples, stomachache, heart pounding. We all have symptoms of frustration, and likely we know them well. Once we identify these symptoms, we can employ conscious breathing to proactively slow down our adrenaline and redirect our thoughts to a constructive choice that serves as a good example to our children rather than to a choice we might regret.

Are we perfect in every moment, always making the right decision? Not likely. As human beings, we'll still find ourselves slipping into negative reactions from time to time. It's in those moments that we must make the choice to give ourselves the space to view the scenario from an objective perspective, think about what happened and how we might have handled it differently (just as we teach our children to do), and then consciously forgive ourselves.

Our reactions don't define us as people, they simply define our choices in the moment. With each new moment comes a new opportunity to make a better choice based on lessons learned and to provide a good example for our little humans.

Mindful Moment

Time: 1–3 minutes
What You Need: A quiet space

1. Close your eyes and think of two positive words that describe you as a parent. Smile.
2. Think of a moment you are not proud of as a parent. Don't feel bad; we all have them. But the point of mindfulness is to be aware and withhold judgment. You can do it.
3. Take a deep breath, and as you breathe out, give yourself a hug. Or, you can imagine yourself in a big circle of pink light.
4. With your next breath, say, "I love myself. I forgive myself. I am doing the best I can."
5. Hug yourself one more time (or find the pink light) and again think of those two positive words.
6. Think of your child and two positive words that describe him or her. Smile.
7. Think of his or her worst moment. Smile.
8. Now, close your eyes and give him or her a hug in your mind.
9. Imagine yourself telling him or her, "I love you. I forgive you. You are doing the best you can."
10. Think of those two positive words. Smile.
11. Repeat to give yourself space and forgiveness the next time you impulsively react as a result of frustration.

CHAPTER 17

This Too Shall Pass

Mindful Reflection

Take a few moments to think about some of the memorable experiences you've had as a parent—the good, the bad, the chaotic, the surprising, the inspirational, and the mundane. They all make up the fabric that is your relationship with your child. Every day of that relationship is different, as is every minute and sometimes every second. The beauty and sometimes the detriment of it all is that it will eventually change. The memories remain, but the moments pass by as time continues on its endless journey.

If you think about it, some of the toughest moments of your life might be some of the fondest memories you look back on. They certainly stick with you as memories not to be forgotten, and they make you the person you are today. The same is true for our days as parents. As we work tirelessly to raise our children and help them learn to stand on their own two feet, the moments are fleeting.

Some moments we want to cherish and never let go, such as hugging our children, listening to them laugh, or watching their excitement when they've accomplished a difficult task. For those moments, we bring ourselves to be fully present to drain every last drop of enjoyment possible.

Some moments are exhausting or even terrifying. For those moments, we can also connect with our breath, find solace in the peace that a simple inhale and exhale can bring, and dig into the many wonderful memories that reside in our heart to help us through the rough times.

We can smile, knowing that this moment will pass and that, as with the nature of duality, another moment of joy will come in due time. For the tough times that are longer than a tantrum, we can use our breath and our mindful awareness to put everything into perspective.

How we feel, what we learn, what we offer and receive from the experience ... these are all fair game for full reflection and, as life would have it, oftentimes a hard lesson. Mindfulness can help us actively perform that reflection and seek out the lesson before the moment fades away. And with that understanding comes peace to weather the storm.

Mindful Moment

Time: 1–3 minutes
What You Need: An intention for awareness in the moment but no need for a quiet space

This exercise is meant to be performed on the spot during a moment that *warms your heart and you wish would never end.*

1. Connect with your breath. Breathe in deeply.
2. Just before you feel your inhale start to become an exhale, notice the slight pause that is innate in the transition. Notice that split second and all the potential that lies within. In that split second, feel your heart opening to fully embrace the moment and capture the potential. Smile.
3. Look into your child's eyes and make eye contact, if possible.
4. Feel the joy of the moment radiating through your heart and connecting with your child's heart, and imprint that feeling with every breath.

1. This exercise is meant to be performed on the spot during a moment that *exhausts, upsets, or frightens you.*
1. Connect with your breath. Breathe in deeply, and consciously choose an extra-long exhale.
2. Think about how you feel in this moment and mentally scan where in your body you feel it.
3. Send your breath to the places where you feel exhaustion, numbness, or tension.
4. Mentally (or physically, if you'd like) hug yourself as you take long, deep breaths and think about what is happening and how you can learn from the experience.
5. With your next deep inhale, think (or whisper, if you're so inclined), *"Everything will be okay."* With your long, slow exhale, think, *"This too shall pass."*
6. Repeat those long breaths for as long as you need.
7. Revisit your body scan. Consider where you feel exhausted, numb, tense, or in need of positive energy.
8. Consciously send your breath and attention to those places. Smile.

CHAPTER 18

Worrying Doesn't Solve Tomorrow's Problems, but It Steals Today's Joy

Mindful Reflection

There's no question that our minds are often busy with planning, managing, and worrying. Mindfulness, meditation, and rest can be good outlets to slow the thoughts and still the mind, but how do we manage negative thoughts or excessive worrying, especially about our beautiful children?

I, for one, am guilty of becoming overwhelmed with worry about my son's safety, especially when he was a newborn. I couldn't stop obsessing about something bad happening to him when I wasn't by his side. It came to a point where it consumed a good majority of my thoughts and wasn't healthy or a positive use of my energy.

So, how did I release these worrisome and oftentimes overly negative thoughts from my mind? I used a mindfulness trick that I'm excited to share with you. I didn't create it, but I'm so grateful that I found it. With practice, it really does work. Here's how.

Mindful Moment

Time: 1–3 minutes
What You Need: An intention for awareness in the moment but no need for a quiet space

1. First, as mentioned with other mindfulness exercises in this book, starting the day with thoughts of gratitude will help set the stage for a positive mind ... "positive mind, positive life." Ending the day with thoughts of gratitude can do the same. Might as well give those bookends a shot and feel the positive thoughts seeping into your day.
2. Throughout your day, as soon as you realize that a negative thought has creeped into your mind, take a deep breath and smile. Yes, that's right, smile. You've caught it. But don't throw it out immediately. Instead, acknowledge it, sit with it for a second, accept it without judgment, and once you feel as though you're at peace with it, consciously release it from your mind, like you're releasing a fish you caught at sea.

The key here is to accept it, instead of resisting it. If you immediately get frustrated with yourself and force the thought quickly out of your mind, you are inviting it to come back with a vengeance. Trust me on this one; I can attest from personal experience. By accepting it, you're taking away its power over you. It's a simple concept but a powerful one. (Try it and see if you agree.)

3. Once you've consciously released the negative thought, take three, slow, deep breaths. With each breath, call a positive thought to your mind. That's three positive thoughts to replace the one negative thought that originally invaded your mind.

4. Over time, the negative thoughts should lessen, leaving space for more peace and positivity. You're welcome!

CHAPTER 19

I Will Not Stress about Things I Cannot Control

Mindful Reflection

The concept of control is one that hit me hard me when I became a parent. Before children, I stressed about things as everyone does, but I felt comfortable in understanding that I was generally the one to feel the impact of my choices.

Parenthood brought a whole new paradigm into play. Now my choices affected the most innocent little creature in the world; a life that depends on my choices for nourishment, love, and safety. That pressure was awe-inspiring and sometimes unbearable.

It wasn't until I stepped back and put into perspective my locus of control that I was able to release myself from things I had no option to control. Then, in turn, I could focus mindfully and patiently on things that could be planned. That release has been lifechanging, as has the self-love I continue to summon, as I remind myself that no one is perfect, not even parents.

Mindful Moment

Time: 3–5 minutes
What You Need: An intention for awareness in the moment and a pencil and paper
Note: It is helpful to repeat this exercise weekly to proactively release stress

1. Grab a pencil and a piece of paper, or open a notepad app on your smartphone. In a pinch, you can simply perform this activity in your head.
2. Take three deep breaths, counting to three on the inhale and four on the exhale. Smile.
3. Write a list of three things that are recurring causes of stress in your life; things that you can generally anticipate will stress you out. Don't think too hard. Immediately write the first three things that pop in your mind. Trust your intuition to generate the list that you need to focus on today.
4. For each item of those three items, write the following.
    a. In three words or less, "why" it stresses you out.

    b.   In one word, the "impact" of or the sacrifice associated with this event (such as money, time, or sanity).

    c.   In two words or less, "whether" you can control it with planning, time, money, or a different perspective.

5.   For those items you can control, write one sentence about how you will prepare to manage or avoid them in the future. Make it as simple as possible.

6.   For those items for which you cannot control no matter what, close your eyes, take a deep breath, and write next to each of them, "I release this stress and accept what is and what will be."

7.   Next, say out loud, or in your mind, "I release this stress and accept what is and what will be."

8.   Take three deep breaths. Feel yourself release that stress in your heart and in your mind.

9.   *Bonus: Bring each of the items you cannot control into a future meditation and think about something good that has or can come from it. It might be a lesson learned or give you a more open mind. Write what you learn and bring that lesson learned to your mind and your heart the next time that uncontrollable event occurs.*

CHAPTER 20

I Am Not Alone in Feeling This Way

Mindful Reflection

If there's one thing you learn throughout this book, or any book on parenting for that matter, it's that many of the same trials and tribulations are shared among parents of all ages, genders, races, and nations. We are all human and, as such, we face many of the same challenges in life, including the challenges that accompany parenting, like fewer hours of sleep, stress in managing frustration outbursts (from our children or from ourselves), fear of maintaining our children's safety, and too many others to name.

The point is, you are not alone in feeling what you're feeling, and that can be a comfort. But how can you find that sense of community and solace in the moment using mindfulness? One way is to bring yourself back into the oneness that makes us all human, rather than seeing yourself as separate from the rest of the human race. We all love; we all fear; we all experience a gamut of emotions in any given day. Just remembering that can be a solace.

Mindful Moment

Time: 5 minutes
What You Need: A public place with time to be thoughtful (preferably not when you've got children to look after at the moment)

1. Start with finding your breath and bringing yourself into the present moment.
2. Notice your body and any feelings that might be hiding—frustration, hopelessness, fearfulness, excitement, or exhaustion. What else can you feel in your body? Can you feel your feet touching the ground? Your arms brushing against passersby? Your hair, clothes, or other belongings moving as you walk?
3. Then, with the next conscious breath in, find the face of someone around you. With the exhale, take a second to imagine what he or she is feeling. This can be a fun exercise for a minute or so of breathing.

4. *Suggestion: Try not to stare at one person continuously for the entire minute, as this can be a little creepy for the person being observed.*
5. Then, with the next minute of breaths, notice the interactions of the people around you. Are they friendly and supporting each other? Are they in a hurry? Do you sense caring? Frustration? Love? Impatience? Try not to take on any of the emotions that might be emitted from those around you, especially if you're an empath. Instead, observe, acknowledge, accept, and release them, as you would any other thought floating through your mind during a meditation.
6. For the next minute, silently send out love to those around you. A good way to do this is to imagine a pink light emitting from your heart and surrounding those around you. That pink light can fill the room or the whole building or an even larger space. Silently offer love to those around you who might need it in this moment.
7. Finally, in the next minute of breath, send yourself gratitude for taking the time to understand and practice this mantra and to send love to those around you, even if they aren't aware of it. With this effort, you are acknowledging the community of consciousness that is humanity while accepting your power to share love and light with yourself and others as a means of lifting the common spirit.

CHAPTER 21

My Feelings Do Not Define Me

Mindful Reflection

As a human, it's important not to forget that feelings are part of reality but do not define us as people or as parents. Feelings are incredibly important for many reasons, not the least of which is that they guide us to understand which emotions we are experiencing.

Fully experiencing and processing emotions is critical to mental health and can even affect physical health. For example, if we feel hopeless or down, we might be experiencing the emotion of sadness. Or, if we feel tense and jumpy, we might be experiencing the emotion of fear. Understanding and processing our emotional states is a key component of mindfulness.

Mindful Moment

Time: 5–10 minutes
What You Need: An intention for awareness and courage to fully process any emotions that come up
Note: This is an activity you can play with your kids like a game; it can help build emotional intelligence

1. As you begin, breathe in and tell yourself, "Everything will be okay." Then, on your breath out, smile.
2. Close your eyes and take a scan of your body and mind. Are there symptoms of feelings in your body or in your thoughts? For example, a feeling of anxiety might cause butterflies in your stomach.
3. Once you've identified a feeling, think about what you need to fully process it. For example, if you feel happily excited, then jumping up and down and screaming "yes!" can help you fully process that positive emotional state. Or, if you feel numb or lonely, you might be experiencing sadness. A hug from a good friend (or child!) might help, or even talking to someone about your feelings might help. Or, it might be best to just sit with the emotion; allow yourself to feel it fully, accept it, and release it.

4. *Bonus: It might take a long time to find all the feelings, understand them, and fully process the emotions. It is recommended to make this exercise a daily or weekly practice to ensure hidden feelings don't go too long without being identified and processed.*

5. Don't forget, each time you identify a feeling and process an emotion, know that you are better off because of it but not defined by the feelings and emotions that have been addressed. *You* are love, and that will never change.

CHAPTER 22

I Have Everything I Need Right Now

Mindful Reflection

At times, the responsibilities that come with parenting can be a lot to manage. It's during those times that we can easily fall into the "if only" mindset. "If only I had more time." Or, "If only I had more money." The "if only" list can continue if we don't take a minute to pause and be mindful of all the wonderful things we *do* have already.

Most important, beyond the "things" we have, we can pause to give thanks for the family and friends we are lucky to have in our lives. Before we know it, we're reminded of all our blessings. Perspective is restored. And, we can feel a "shift" in our perspective of what is truly important to us. That is the power of being mindful … and grateful.

Mindful Moment

Time: 3–5 minutes
What You Need: A quiet space and possibly a vase with flowers

1. Take a minute to pause your current "if only" thought. Be sure not to scold yourself or to push the thought away. Instead, take a deep breath in and simply acknowledge the thought as though it's a visitor coming over for dinner. Feel free to serve it an appetizer (acknowledge it), but make a conscious effort not to let it stay for dinner (by becoming entrenched in the "if only" mindset). On your exhale, feel yourself releasing the thought as though it is a weight off your shoulders.

2. Now, close your eyes and find a comfortable seat. Take a moment to feel the love in your heart—the source of your inner peace. This is a true sense of love for yourself, for your family, for your friends and acquaintances, for humankind, and for Mother Earth. Let that sense of love fill your heart, like water filling a vase. Smile.

3. Next, take a moment to think of each of the people (and pets!) in your life whom you love and those who love you. *Suggestion: You can also add people who might be difficult but mean well or who help you learn the hard lessons in life.* Imagine putting an imaginary flower in the imaginary vase as a symbol of the loving relationships you are blessed with. Smile.

4. Next, take an inventory of all the important lessons you've learned, the subjects you've studied, the capabilities you've developed, the people you've served, the places you've visited, and the accomplishments you've made through hard work. Give thanks for taking the time, money, energy, and intention to earn and experience each one. As you do, imagine putting another flower in that imaginary vase full of water as a symbol of your dedicated effort to becoming the person you are today. Smile.

5. Then, take a moment to think of the things in your life that bring you comfort or joy. For example, a warm bed, a full pantry, or even your favorite outfit. Acknowledge anything that comes up and accept it without evaluation. This is another flower to add to your imaginary vase. Smile.

6. Finally, imagine the moments of parenthood that make it all worth it. Feel the hugs, hear the laughs, and see the happy eyes and smiles. Let that flower be the brightest in the vase. Smile.

7. With a full heart and an imaginary vase full of beautiful flowers, take a deep breath in and feel your perspective "shift" to a true understanding of what really makes you happy. As you exhale, tell yourself, "I have everything I need."

8. *Bonus: Use a real vase and flowers as you perform this exercise for the first time. In the future, when you feel the "if only" mindset coming on, take a minute to "smell the roses."*

CHAPTER 23

Good Enough Is Enough for Now

Mindful Reflection

This might be the most important statement a parent can think of on any given day. Balancing kids, love, friends, family, home, work, hobbies, and all the other details in life is more than a full-time job. It is virtually impossible to be at your best for everything day in and day out, much less solely for your job as a parent.

A happy day often starts with a mindset of acceptance that "perfect" is not always possible and "good enough" will be enough to take good care of your family *and* maintain your sanity. But how can you keep yourself on track with that mindset throughout the day? Mindfulness to the rescue once again.

Mindful Moment

Time: 1–3 minutes
What You Need: An intention for a mindful check-in at the beginning of the day or before a daunting situation

1. As the day begins, with a few deep breaths, give yourself a mental hug, while consciously welcoming the thought that "good enough" is enough and anything else is bonus. It might help to envision hugging yourself or even a pair of wings wrapping around you in comfort.
2. When it's time to start important and often exhausting tasks, like mealtimes, bath times, or bedtimes, take a deep breath and remind yourself once again that you're aiming for good enough. Once again, visualize a comforting hug.
3. Once you've thoroughly embraced the "good enough" mindset, don't forget to smile; it can change your mindset in a millisecond.
4. This exercise wouldn't be complete without taking a moment of gratitude at the end of each day for your efforts, even if they were "good enough" and not perfect. Give thanks for the energy and physical abilities that carried you through even the toughest tasks, and the positive mental perspective that offered peace of mind when disappointment could have set in—"good enough is enough for now."

CHAPTER 24

Mistakes Are on the Path of Creation

Mindful Reflection

The path of parenting isn't easy, isn't straight, and certainly isn't the same for any two parents. Since there's no one-size-fits-all manual, we can just do the best we can. Mistakes are inherent, and that's one of the most powerful realizations one can make, *must* make, to preserve sanity. However, learning from those mistakes is critical, just as it is for any mistake in life.

One of my favorite ways to use mindfulness is to reflect on a mistake by meditating on it. Stay with me here. This does not mean beating yourself up for several minutes and finishing with an even greater sense of self-defeat.

Instead, the point is to create space for ourselves to observe our own behavior, find the lesson to be learned, and be grateful to ourselves for taking the time to do so. It is with this practice of mindful meditation that we can stay on our path without having to take that crossroads again.

Mindful Exercise

Time: 5–10 minutes
What You Need: A quiet space
Note: This meditation involves visualization, so closing your eyes can help or softening your gaze to focus on a spot with minimal distraction. It's also recommended to perform this meditation at least a few hours, if not a full day, after making a "mistake," so as to create space for objective reflection

1. Find your natural breath and allow your body to relax. Permit yourself to forget about the mistake for a minute and focus on the present moment.
2. Starting with your toes, squeeze them as you deeply inhale, and slowly relax them completely on an audible exhale. Proceed to gently tense and relax your body, following with your legs, belly, arms, hands, shoulders, jaw, and eyes. Feel your body relaxing completely, and, as you do, maintain a cadence of steady, conscious breathing.

3. Bring to mind the incident during which the mistake was made. Be sure not to assess blame or judgment. Instead, simply see the scene before you as though you are an audience member at a play. As each part of the scene unfolds, make note of what happened, how it made you feel, and where in your body each feeling resides.
4. Make note of any major emotions that arise during the scene- that is, sadness, anger, fear.
5. At the end of the scene, take a minute to sit quietly and think about what you might have done differently if you were to replay that scene in real life. How might you help yourself create space, in the moment, by taking deep breaths or even stepping back to assess and make a more thoughtful decision about how you might react—or mindfully respond—in the moment?
6. Then, take a minute to think about how you might feel, and how your family might feel, if you took that alternative approach in the future.
7. Lastly, and certainly not least, think about the emotions you noted earlier in step 4. Find the place in your body where you felt them, and with compassion send your breath and your focus to that part of the body.
8. Sit with your breath for a brief time while conjuring the thoughts, "I love myself. I accept myself. I am doing the best I can."
9. Once you have addressed each of those emotions and have accepted each with your breath and focus, take a minute to send yourself gratitude for taking the time to perform this exercise. You are making the conscious decision to learn from your mistakes and to create a more mindful and positive life for you and your family. That is something to be grateful for and proud of.

Section III: Inspiration

"Sometimes we're tested not to show our weaknesses,
but to discover our strengths."

—*Unknown*

INSPIRATION

Parenthood can be the most rewarding and blissful experience at times. At other times, it can feel like a minefield of challenges meant to test our patience and compassion. It is at those times that mindfulness can be the most valuable, free, ever-present tool we have.

It is at those times that we can allow ourselves to make the *choice* to be calm and grounded in order to respond thoughtfully and lovingly. It is in those times that we can *choose* to be the best version of ourselves for our families and, most important, for ourselves.

CHAPTER 25

I Choose Calm

Mindful Reflection

Remaining calm when parenting can sometimes seem like an impossible feat, especially when you're the only one who seems to be consciously trying to do so. However, choosing calm can do wonders for our mental state and for our ability to make sound decisions and to provide a positive example for our children in times of stress. Indeed, our children sense our reactions to stress, even when we don't realize it.

Believe it or not, you don't have to hide in a quiet corner to find calm; you can find it in every moment in every place and time, if you use the right tools. Controlled breathing, or pranayama, has the ability to transform the mental state quickly, quietly, and effectively. And, the best part about using pranayama to find calmness in the moment is that your breath is always available. It doesn't cost anything to use it, and you can use it as a calming technique, generally, without anyone else even knowing.

This free, portable, and effective tool can help you create space in the moment, once you've identified that your stress signals— tense jaw, gripping hands, short breath, etc.—have been activated. By practicing pranayama daily, you can create a powerful habit that will give you the space you need in stressful situations to reset and make the choice to remain calm.

Mindful Moment

Time: 1–3 minutes
What You Need: A quiet space
Note: An easy form of pranayama that you can use in a pinch—even without others knowing that you're doing it—is sahita kumbhaka, which is a form of controlled breathing involving cessation of breath after the inhalation and after the exhalation. It can also be effective to extend the exhale, which engages the parasympathetic nervous system to assist in reducing anxiety and stress. Combining these two pranayama techniques with some mindful mantras can be a powerful exercise to help you choose calm

The first time you practice this exercise, you'll likely want to try it when you have a few minutes for yourself. But, with some practice, you can use it in the moment, as needed.

1. Begin with a few deep breaths, in through your nose and out through your mouth.
2. Once you feel that your focus is in the present moment, begin breathing in and out deeply through your nose, and bring your inhale and exhale each to a three count. Stay here for a few breaths, simply focusing on your counting, inhaling for three and exhaling for three.
3. Once you are in a rhythm, introduce your sahita kumbhaka by adding a three-count pause after your inhale and another three-count pause after your exhale. As you pause, allow your shoulders and jaw to relax, rather than tensing as though you're holding your breath under water.
4. Next, add the mindful mantra "I choose calm" on the inhale, and "I am calm" on the exhale. You can stay here for a minute or so and then increase the exhale count to four and eventually to five, if possible. Fairly quickly, you should feel your body relax and your energy reset. Enjoy a clearer mind and a calmer mindset!

CHAPTER 26

I Choose to Radiate a Positive Attitude

Mindful Reflection

As human beings, we are bound to experience highs and lows in life, and those feelings are bound to affect our attitude. However, consciously manifesting a positive attitude each day can help us enjoy each moment and support more positive experiences with our families.

Mindfulness can help us use our imagination and our senses to cultivate the warm, positive energy the sun can have on our body and use that feeling to conjure a positive attitude on the spot.

Mindful Moment

Time: 1–3 minutes
What You Need: A quiet space is helpful, but with some practice, this can be practiced in the moment as needed

1. Take a long, deep breath to bring yourself to the present moment.
2. Think of the first word that describes your attitude at the moment. It should be the first word that comes to mind, even if it's silly or negative.
3. Smile and say silently or out loud, "I accept myself," as you acknowledge and accept your current attitude. Try not to place judgment on how you are feeling or the attitude you are holding at this moment.
4. Take another deep breath and say, "I release my current attitude and make space for a positive attitude."
5. Next, think of the best day you can remember with your family. As you do, imagine holding a positive attitude in your heart, just like a sun radiating warmth and positive energy.
6. Take another deep breath and imagine yourself feeling that warmth and positive energy throughout your whole body, starting with your toes, ankles, legs, hips, belly, heart, shoulders, arms, hands, throat, face, and the crown of your head.

7. Hold this energy throughout your body as you say, "I radiate a positive attitude."
8. Take three more slow, deep breaths, and then smile.
9. If you need to quickly bring yourself back to this feeling throughout the day, simply take a deep breath, remember the warm feeling of the positive attitude, and say, "I radiate a positive attitude."

CHAPTER **27**

I Choose Empathy

Mindful Reflection

Empathy is a virtue worthy of becoming a lifelong habit. With greater screen time comes fewer face-to-face interactions and, as such, fewer opportunities to "connect" with others through empathy. Now more than ever, it is critical to practice empathy during interactions with our family and to teach them how to do the same.

Practicing empathy entails being fully present to understand someone else's suffering by seeking to understand their perspectives and the associated emotions. As with any virtuous skill, it takes practice to integrate empathy into your life as a habit.

The following mindfulness exercise is meant to be performed in the moment with your child when he or she is experiencing frustration or suffering; however, it can be visualized, performed alone in silence, or performed with someone other than your child, as needed.

Mindful Moment

Time: 3–5 minutes (or more as the situation requires)
What You Need: An intention for awareness in the moment but no need for a quiet space
Note: This mindful moment is also something you can teach your children as they learn about empathy

1. Just as you might do when sitting down for meditation, give yourself permission to be present without judgment. Take a deep breath in, as you ground yourself in the moment. *Suggestion: If it helps, you can imagine your feet growing roots into the ground to physically "ground" yourself.*

2. Continue to breathe as you create space to actively listen. With each breath in, take in the sound and feeling of what's being communicated to you. With each breath out, release any desire to instantly correct the situation or respond. Simply create space to listen.

3. As it feels appropriate, consciously put yourself in your child's shoes. Seek to understand, not to judge. Seek also to remain as objective as possible, rather than allowing yourself to be overcome with your child's emotions. Briefly imagine what it feels like to be experiencing the situation from the child's perspective—physically, mentally, and emotionally. How might the experience feel different from your child's shoes than from yours? This will allow you to make an honest connection with your child.

4. With an open heart, again ground yourself in the present moment with your breath. As you do, remind yourself that you are here to be supportive and empathetic. That doesn't mean you have to solve the problem. It simply means you are available for support and offering empathy from a place of love and trust.

CHAPTER 28

I Choose to Be Present with Myself and Others

Mindful Reflection

Life has a tendency to move fast, especially if we're focused on frantically checking items off our to-do list. Being a parent means balancing a dozen or more things above and beyond our own needs. However, that doesn't mean we have to let life fly by without savoring the moments that make it special.

I heard a quote by Theodor Seuss Geisel (Dr. Seuss) that really puts it into perspective. "Sometimes you will never know the value of a moment until it becomes a memory." What if we're living in the "good old days" but not taking the time to enjoy life? But how can we enjoy life when it moves so fast and furious? How can we stop and experience the moment when we barely have enough time to sleep or to take time for ourselves?

It's possible to feel the value of a moment *and* accomplish the important things on your list. The secret is to intentionally create space in the moment by grounding yourself and using your senses to thoroughly experience all that life has to offer. Before you know it, life moves more slowly with greater ease and greater meaning.

Mindful Moment

Time: 1–3 minutes
What You Need: An intention for awareness in the moment but no need for a quiet space
Note: This is a good mindfulness exercise to share with your family

1. Start by taking a deep breath in, pausing for a second at the top, and then releasing your breath slowly. Let your body fully relax and your mind become more still as you continue with conscious breathing.
2. Imagine creating an extra space in time to enjoy everything the current moment has to offer, as though you're moving through quicksand. Give yourself permission to release any immediate desire to fast forward to the next moment in time. *Suggestion: If you're with your family, you might consider walking them through the next steps to also experience the moment with their senses.*

3. Feel the ground below your feet (or your seat, if you're sitting) supporting you in this moment. Take note of any other places where your body has contact with the ground or an object.

4. Listen for any sounds that might be floating around and through your eardrums. Did you notice these sounds before?

5. Allow yourself to take in the smells around you. If you can't smell anything in particular, enjoy the crisp, clean air running through your nostrils as you breathe in.

6. Acknowledge if you have a taste in your mouth. If you're eating or drinking, bring your movements to slow motion as you gently savor the experience.

7. Finally, scan the space around you. Who or what is a part of this moment with you? Is there anything around you that you hadn't noticed before?

8. Now, in a few simple words, articulate what is happening in this moment. What is the value of this moment? Is it a new experience? Is it time shared with a loved one? Is it a difficult moment with a lesson just begging to be learned or a hurdle just waiting to be overcome? Or is it one of the more ordinary moments in life that so often go unnoticed?

9. Take another deep breath in, pause at the top to smile, and then release your breath as you release the moment.

CHAPTER 29

I Am the Master of My Response to Challenges

Mindful Reflection

As parents, we want the best for our children. But that can often lead to setting high expectations for them and for ourselves, even when those expectations aren't realistic. High expectations breed pressure, which can make it overwhelming to manage the inevitable challenges that accompany parenthood.

In the moments when we feel overpowered by life's challenges or by our own expectations, mindfulness and self-compassion can be game changers. It's in those moments that mindfulness can support our choice to briefly create space with the situation at hand and *respond* based on reflection and compassion rather than *react* based on impulse or emotion.

The goal of this exercise is to cultivate an understanding about what triggers you and then to give yourself the space you need to respond thoughtfully. Over time, you'll find this mindfulness and grounding becoming second nature, and eventually your habitual response will shift more permanently.

Mindful Moment

Time: 1–3 minutes
What You Need: An intention for awareness and reflection in the moment
Note: This is a simple exercise to teach older children, especially teenagers, to manage their responses

1. First, pause and breathe. In that conscious breath, intentionally relieve yourself of the initial impulse to get frustrated or impulsive. Remind yourself that it's okay to pause, even when time is ticking for a response.
2. Then, take several slow, deep breaths to ground yourself in your senses.
3. Consider what you are feeling at the moment. Can you identify your trigger? Is your heart racing? Palms sweaty? Teeth gritting? Fists clenched? That sense of self can help ground you in the moment and help you better

understand how your body and your energy are managing the situation. It's important not to place judgment on yourself while taking a scan of your senses. Be a silent observer, but don't judge.

4. Then, take another few deep, slow breaths for good measure, as you slowly relax your eyes, jaw, neck, shoulders, fists, stomach, legs, calves, and toes. These are the usual offenders causing tension in the body. Be sure to include any other areas of the body that tend to hold tension for you or any place in your body that needs more focus based on your body scan in step 3.

5. Once you're grounded and more relaxed, do something you might never have thought to do in this situation ... smile. Yes, allow yourself to smile and thank yourself for taking a second to pause rather than release an emotional, stress-filled outburst that might have negatively affected you, your family, your day, or more.

6. Now, think the words *respond thoughtfully,* as you breathe in deeply. With the exhale, consider how you might respond mindfully rather than react impulsively.

7. *Suggestion: You can also touch your heart, watch, bracelet, or anything else that is special to you and that can serve a personal reminder to you to "respond thoughtfully" in the moment.*

CHAPTER 30

Patience Is a Gift... Enjoy the Pause

Mindful Reflection

Patience is perspective. At least that's how I've perceived it since becoming a parent. Before I had a child, my priorities were aligned differently, often to fitting more into a shorter period of time. After having a child, I realized that my priorities had changed and that my day was often taken off course to a set of completely unplanned events.

Planning was often a futile exercise, and my patience was tested like never before. Trust me, it took time to change my perspective to allow myself to flow and find patience in circumstances that did not go according to my battle-tested planning skills. But, I realized quickly that an ounce of patience could get me to where I needed to be much more calmly and effectively than sheer force of will had served me in the past.

I started to find myself seeking times when I had to pause and be patient, even if only because it was an opportunity to pause in an otherwise crazy day. It was almost a gift to be forced to slow down and be mindful rather than rushing through everything. It was at those times when I really became aware of myself, my feelings, and my surroundings. And that's when I made some of my most profound realizations.

How can it be a gift when something is not going as planned and you're forced to slow down, you ask? Well, consider it an extra moment in your day that you had not planned for, when you can give yourself permission to breathe and just be. Not *do*. Just *be*.

Mindful Moment

Time: 1–3 minutes
What You Need: An intention to pause, breathe, and think about how you're feeling in the moment
Note: This is something you can share with your children. It can be fun to practice at a stoplight or in line at the grocery store

1. First, come to your breath by taking a few deep breaths in through your nose and out through your mouth.
2. Start to think about how you're feeling. Do you have any emotions that have welled up and are in need of processing? Are you carrying tension or pain in your body that you can work out with some focused breath?
3. Now, begin noticing your thoughts. What's going on in your mind at the moment? Is there a song playing in your head that you hadn't noticed? Any stray thoughts passing through that you can acknowledge and release?
4. Next, give notice to your surroundings. What's going on in the space around you? Anything you didn't notice before? Anything strange or awkward or even amusing to take note of?
5. Once you're ready to move on and no longer have the need for the gift of a pause in your day, take a second to smile. Think about what you noticed. Thank yourself for taking advantage of that moment rather than getting frustrated.

CHAPTER 31

All You Can Do Is the Best You Can Do, and the Best You Can Do Is Enough

Mindful Reflection

This mantra is near and dear to my heart, as my dad used to say it to me all the time when I was growing up. It gave me the inspiration to do my best at anything I decided to take on. But, it also enabled me to accept that I can't control everything in life and to be okay with knowing that my "best" in that project, or that day, or even in that moment would be enough to see progress, even if things didn't work out exactly as planned.

This mantra has also been exceptionally helpful to me as a parent. There are so many factors out of our control as parents; even the most controlling person has to eventually admit that getting stressed about every piece of the puzzle that makes up parenthood is futile. A powerful mantra like this can be a great tool to remind us of that truth and relieve us of the burden of being the "perfect" parent.

Mindful Moment

Time: 1–3 minutes
What You Need: It's helpful to have a quiet space, but this can also be used in the moment, as needed

1. Before you begin a new task, take a second to pause and breathe deeply. Allow yourself to come to the present moment with intention.
2. Say, "All you can do is the best you can do, and the best you can do is enough."
3. Take another deep breath to acknowledge that your "best" today might be different from your "best" yesterday, based on your energy level, your time parameters, or even factors out of your control, like an unexpected interruption. Allow yourself the space to accept that and continue with a positive mindset.
4. Take another deep breath and thank yourself for all the hard work you are about to offer to this task. Then, proceed to conquer the task with this gratitude as encouragement.

5. As you finish the task, take a second to reflect mindfully about what you accomplished, how you feel, and how others might feel who have been affected by your hard work.
6. Finally, once again, give yourself a smile and a moment of gratitude. Consciously remind yourself, "I am enough."

CHAPTER 32

Be Strong Enough to Stand Alone, Smart Enough to Know When You Need Help, and Brave Enough to Ask for It

Mindful Reflection

You can be the bravest, smartest, and even calmest person in the room and still feel overwhelmed under the load of responsibilities that accompanies parenthood and, let's face it, "adulting." Sometimes it helps to have a reminder that you *can* ask for help. Or, sometimes you just need to believe that you can give yourself permission to ask for help when you need it.

For many, it isn't easy to overcome the fear or ego associated with allowing someone to take a portion of the burden off your shoulders. But, by pausing and considering where in your life you could use help, your family and your sanity will thank you. In the end, that decision could be the bravest and smartest thing you do for your family.

Mindful Moment

Time: 5–10 minutes
What You Need: A quiet space and a pencil and paper

1. Start with taking a deep breath to bring yourself to the present moment. You can do this by running a scan of your senses. What do you see, hear, smell, and taste at the moment? How do you feel at this moment?
2. With the next deep breath, take a scan of the major responsibilities that make up your week. Try to limit it to the top five to ten.
3. For each responsibility or critical task identified, assign it to one of two buckets: (1) "Yes, I've got this," or, (2) "I could use some help." (A third bucket, titled "911, HELP NEEDED STAT," is also an option, if needed.)

   This is a great time to use the power of self-awareness to identify where you could use support. For instance, a good way to determine which bucket a task might fit in is to be *aware* of how you feel when you think of the task. If you feel relaxed or connected to your heart, or even if you feel nothing in particular, it's probably best to drop it in the first bucket. On the other hand, if you feel your breath quicken, a tightening of the throat, or tenseness in the pit of your stomach, you probably want to put it in the second bucket.

4. After your scan, take an inventory of the second bucket. For those items, you could use some relief if you had a little help or even greater planning. Now, visualization and intuition become valuable tools to help you understand what kind of support would be helpful.

   For each of those tasks, one by one, imagine that they are in a package that you breathe in and send to your heart. Once in your heart center, take a few breaths while you imagine how you can garner support and from whom. Maybe someone's face pops into your mind, or maybe you feel inspired to make a list of steps to better prepare for that task. Whatever comes to you first, trust your intuition, and show your bravery and compassion for yourself by asking for help. This exercise can be helpful if repeated when you start to feel overwhelmed or even on a regular basis as a periodic planning tool.

5. *Bonus: You can also use visualization to plan how to ask for support. To do so, spend a few minutes meditating on the face or the energy of the person or people who can help you with a task in the second bucket. Allow your intuition to bring up any words that feel appropriate when asking for assistance. Send a pink light from your heart to their heart and back to yourself to make the connection of compassion and self-love that will be helpful as you put aside your ego and use your courage to ask for the support you need.*

CHAPTER 33

Each Struggle Reveals a New Strength

Mindful Reflection

You might think that life begins outside your comfort zone. But even if you're not stretching your boundaries daily, life has a way of bringing you through struggles virtually every day, especially when you're raising a child. One's perspective on these struggles can mean the difference between frustration, desperation, and inspiration.

This mantra "Each struggle reveals a new strength" can be incredibly powerful, because it gives you the opportunity to find the gift that can come only from struggle ... a lesson learned and oftentimes renewed strength. This isn't always easy to discover for everyday struggles, but it's possible. Mindfulness can help unlock that inspirational perspective with the simple trick of personifying your intuition.

Mindful Moment

Time: 3–5 minutes
What You Need: It's helpful to have a quiet space, but this can also be used in the moment, as needed

1. First, pause and find your breath. Take a deep breath in and acknowledge the current situation as a struggle. Accept it as it is, without judgment. As you breath out, consciously release the frustration that comes with that struggle.
2. *Insight: It often takes many breaths with this intention to begin to feel a release. This will take patience.*
3. Once you've reached a place where your breath is calmer and your mind is still, imagine there's a little person (maybe your childhood self or maybe a fictional person, whatever is most comfortable) on your shoulder observing the situation without judgment. Take a minute as this little person to answer the following questions, with the intent to accept the first answer that comes to mind for each, spending no more than thirty seconds on each.

Remember not to assign blame or place judgment as you answer these questions.

- What is the struggle?
- Who is involved?
- Why did the struggle begin?
- Why is it continuing?
- Is there a way to use compromise, love, or acceptance to overcome the struggle?

4. Once you have thought through each of the answers with honesty, think about why this struggle might have occurred—not who started it and how, as you thought of in step 2—explore the greater reason for the struggle. Is there a lesson to be learned here? Is there a reason you have endured this experience? Think of what this struggle has taught you or how it has inspired you. *Insight: It might take several conscious breaths to understand the lesson or inspiration, or it might be something you let sit for a while and allow to come up when it's ready.*

5. Once you feel as though you truly understand the gift that the struggle has brought, smile ... for that is the gift of understanding you can keep in your memory and possibly even teach your children.

6. Before you finish and go about your day, take a minute to offer gratitude to the little person on your shoulder for offering an unbiased observation. Smile ... this little person is always there to help you find that unbiased perspective and reveal those gifts of understanding whenever needed.

CHAPTER 34

Each New Day Is an Opportunity to Start Fresh

Mindful Reflection

If only we took the time to appreciate the unique opportunity each new day brings. We have 1,440 minutes every day to cherish and to devote to the care of ourselves, our households, our family, and our dreams. But sometimes the to-do lists we create for ourselves are overwhelming, or the memory of yesterday's stress weighs heavily on our minds. That is part of being human. But, it doesn't have to be the only part.

By taking a few moments at the beginning of each day to consciously visualize how we plan to use the next 1,440 minutes, we can mindfully set the tone that today is a chance to start fresh and proactively create the sense of power and spirit of joy that can help us overcome the worries that linger or the to-do list that haunts us.

Mindful Moment

Time: 3–5 minutes
What You Need: A few moments of peace as you wake up in the morning
Note: This meditation uses the powerful forces of visualization to support the manifestation of positive outcomes

1. As you wake up, take a long, deep breath, and pause momentarily at the top of the inhale to smile. On the exhale, say, "Thank you for a new day."
2. With each of your next three deep breaths, give gratitude for three things that bring you joy, such as spending time with your beautiful family or even the opportunity to try something new.
3. Next, take about thirty seconds to set an intention for your experience today. In one or two clear sentences, how would you like to feel today, and what would you like to accomplish?
4. Now to begin the powerful exercise of visualization. Take a few minutes to visualize each hour of your day.

- How would you like the day to start?
- What sort of attitude are you bringing to each of your planned activities?
- What types of interactions would you like to have with others?
- Are there any goals you'd like to achieve?

Imagine yourself performing each of the key interactions and achieving your goals with intention. Don't forget to visualize how you'd like your day to end, down to the second that you lay your head on the pillow to get a good night's sleep.

5. Finally, take another deep breath in, smile at the top, and with your exhale say, "Let's do this."
6. *Suggestion: Visualization becomes even more effective when coupled with journaling. Once you visualize your intentions for the day, take a minute or two to journal about your top few goals and how you'd like to feel throughout the day.*

CHAPTER 35

Be the Parent Today That You Want Your Children to Remember Tomorrow

Mindful Reflection

I've mentioned throughout this book that our behaviors and reactions (or, preferably, "thoughtful responses") serve as examples for our children. That's not to place pressure on parents, as we're certainly not perfect, but instead to give us encouragement to *be* the person we'd like our children to look up to and emulate. Even through the process of making a mistake, we can help them understand our process for seeking to understand, acknowledge, accept, and release it as we learn from our mistakes and forgive ourselves.

But how can we become conscious of the example we're setting for our children? How can we embrace the opportunity to *be* a positive force in their lives instead of crumbling under the pressure? Mindfulness can help us, as can love and acceptance for ourselves and our children just as we are.

Mindful Exercise

Time: 3–5 minutes
What You Need: It's helpful to have a quiet space
Note: We can also teach our children about this process to help them embody the type of example they'd like to set for their siblings or peers

1. First, take a deep, conscious breath in through your nose. Release an audible exhale through your mouth. As you do so, give yourself a hug to show acceptance and self-love just as you are.
2. Next, use your five senses to come to the present moment and seek to understand how you are feeling in this moment. What do you see, smell, hear, taste, and feel in this moment? As you do so, think about how the answers to these questions reflect the person you are *being* or *becoming*.
3. Next, sit for a minute and meditate or breathe, thinking about the person you are bringing to the world each day.

Is there a word or two you'd use to describe that person? Is there a word or two you'd use to describe the impact you're having on yourself, your family, and the world around you? It's critical to be honest but also show self-love throughout this process. Remind yourself that no one is perfect and that you're doing the best you can.

4. At the end of that minute, take a few deep, conscious breaths and think about the vision you have of yourself and your life. How does that vision align (or possibly not align) with the energy and attitude you're bringing to the world, as you mentally noted in step 3? Where can you see alignment? Where you can offer yourself space to make new choices? Consider thinking of a word or a gesture that will help you remember your vision and the choices you are making to bring that vision to life. You can always come back to that word or gesture at the beginning of the day or at times when you are ready to make a decision that will affect you, your family, and the world.

5. Finally, take a minute of deep breathing to fill your body with a sense of gratitude and love. If gratitude is not available to you at the moment, then simply seek to accept yourself as you are and share love for yourself through your breath.

CHAPTER 36

Be the Change You Want to See in the World

Mindful Reflection

Beyond our role as parents, we are citizens of Earth with the opportunity to make a positive impact on our communities and beyond. Whether through our vocation, our avocation, or simply the way we interact with those around us, each moment offers the potential to make the world a better place.

Whether we realize it or not, our children look to us to set an example for how to treat ourselves, other people, and the environment. Becoming intentional with our actions and mindful of their impacts can influence our experiences in life, and it can guide our children's behavior and, in doing so, create a lasting impact on our world for generations to come.

Mindful Moment

Time: 1–3 minutes
What You Need: A quiet space and a pencil and paper

1. First, come to the present by taking a few deep, conscious breaths. Allow yourself to step outside the demands of the day and find sanctuary in a peaceful moment.
2. Next, grab a pencil and a piece of paper. Write a positive change you'd like to see in the world. For instance, world peace. (Go big, right?) The topic isn't important, but ensure it's something that resonates with your heart.
3. Then, write two to three words you believe support this change. For example, compassion, love, and patience.
4. For each of those words, write one thing you can do each day to make that word actionable. For example, for the word compassion, it could mean listening to someone who is having a bad day and offering a hug.
5. Revisit this list as often as needed to remind yourself of how to embody positive changes. Share stories with your family about the steps you've taken toward positively affecting the world. Encourage conversations with your children about how they too can join in. Ask for their ideas about how to do so.

6. *Bonus: The next time you meditate, focus on one of the three words you wrote about supporting positive change in the world. Be open to the thoughts, ideas, and inner wisdom that emerge.*

ABOUT THE AUTHOR

Angela Wolf is a proud mother, meditation teacher, and founder of Meditot, a children's meditation and mindfulness academy based in Denver, Colorado. She enjoys learning about and practicing mindfulness and meditation, hiking, yoga, and spending time with her family, who continues to bring her joy with each passing moment.

Photo Credit: Butterscotch Rose Photography

Made in the USA
Coppell, TX
11 January 2021